SAFE
SEX

BY HARVEY FIERSTEIN

Safe Sex (1987)
Torch Song Trilogy (1981)

Harvey Fierstein's

*

SAFE

SEX

Atheneum / New York

Photographs by Peter Cunningham

Printed in the United States of America

For my darling Court Miller

Sex is good. It is not wrongful or unhealthful. AIDS has blinded us from this simple truth. It has poisoned the joy of affection. It has banished the spontaneity of loving. It imbues lovers with guilt, strangers with distrust, and victims with shame. I curse this disease and any viruslike person who would call it God given. I mourn for the promised lives it has stolen and exalt those now fighting for their right to live.

These plays are dedicated not only to our lost loved ones, but to those who stood bravely by their sides. To all who work toward the annihilation of this threat and to those now threatened.

A special message to my little Christopher: We will live to celebrate life again. Trust me on this one.

For the living and the dead: John Mulkeen, Barbara Colson, Ted Hook, Gary Hunt, Joel Crothers, Ted Azar, David Sommers . . .

Remembering too: Jules and Ann Weiss, Leon and Marilyn Klinghoffer, Lisa and Ilsa Klinghoffer . . .

Safe Sex premiered on January 8, 1987 at the La Mama ETC as part of their twenty-fifth anniversary celebration. The production was subsequently presented by the Shubert Organization at the Lyceum Theater in New York City with a March 19, 1987 first performance with the following cast:

MANNY AND JAKE

MANNY John Mulkeen   JAKE John Wesley Shipp

SAFE SEX

MEAD John Wesley Shipp   GHEE Harvey Fierstein

ON TIDY ENDINGS

MARION Anne De Salvo   JUNE Billie McBride
JIMMY Ricky Addison Reed   ARTHUR Harvey Fierstein

Directed by Eric Concklin

ORIGINAL SCORE Ada Janik

LIGHTING DESIGN Craig Miller

COSTUME DESIGN Nanzi Adzima

SCENERY John Falabella

SCULPTURES Gretchen Green

SOUND Tom Morse

CASTING Jimmy Bohr

PRODUCTION STAGE MANAGER Bob Borod

STAGE MANAGER Glen Gardali

Contents

Preface

Never have I been as conscious of time and its relationship to my work as I am at this moment. After
making casual notes during the summer of 1986, I began
the actual writing of *Safe Sex* in September. The first
drafts were completed in November. January saw their
premiere. And now, in the midst of February, I've been
asked to comment in some way on the plays for purpose
of this publication. How can I? How could I possibly
have any perspective or new insights with so little life
lived between the initial inspiration, the execution and
this reflection. I have not changed in this short time, nor
have the lives of those upon whom I have based my
characters. We are as we were. More than any other
work with which I have involved myself, these plays
are this moment. They could not have existed two years
ago, and probably would not be written two years hence.
So new is the world from which I address you that
nothing in these plays can be assumed common knowledge. So new is the concept of safe or unsafe sex that I
still can't accept its reality. I believe these plays have a
great deal to say about who and what and where we
are. I will leave the dispersal of this information to the
plays themselves without Monday Morning Quarter-
backing. I would like, however, to have you understand
the bizarre sensation I feel as I present this work to you.

Never have I felt so of the moment, so "time-capsu-
lized." Here is what I needed to say today. Here is my
last phone call, the guests just·leaving my home, the
thought I just completed. Herein you will find my world
as it exists. These are my friends and fears. These are
my wants and losses. I hope they mean something to
you. My only wish is that from where you now read
this, in your present moment, this world of mine no
longer exists.

Author's Note

Never lose your sense of humor.

MANNY
AND
JAKE

*

MANNY, *an irresistibly beautiful young man, sits alone on a* white *sofa placed Center Stage.*
HE *holds in Yoga's "lotus" position, but his arms are outstretched, his palms reaching heavenward.* HE *stares glassily skyward.*
HE *is dressed in bright red shirt and pants.* HE *is barefooted.*
JAKE *enters strolling slowly.* HE *too is beautiful, young, irresistible.* HE *is dressed in pink.*
JAKE *sees* MANNY *and is immediately taken with him.*
JAKE *stares, takes a casual look about for eavesdroppers; seeing none,* HE *approaches* MANNY *casually.*
JAKE *coyly crosses in front of him but* MANNY *stares blindly as before.*
JAKE *tries posing in front of* MANNY; HE *flexes and stretches alluringly but to no avail.*
Frustrated, JAKE *wanders away.*
Pause.
JAKE *returns.* HE *strolls once again behind the sofa. No reaction.* HE *strolls in front of the sofa. No reaction.* HE *leans on the sofa. Nothing.* HE *lies across the sofa and still* MANNY *remains unmoved.*
Suddenly JAKE *lunges at* MANNY, *grabbing him by the throat and choking.* MANNY *gags and gasps for air but does not struggle.* HE *remains passionless.*

Exhausted, JAKE *lets go of* MANNY *and regains his composure.* MANNY *restores himself as well.*
JAKE *begins to leave as* MANNY *closes his eyes and speaks:*

MANNY

Talk.

(JAKE *stops and looks back*)

JAKE

You say something?

(*No reply. No movement.* JAKE *cautiously reapproaches*)

JAKE

What're you doing?

MANNY

Praying for sex.

JAKE

Praying?

MANNY

Uh huh.

JAKE

For sex?

MANNY

Uh huh.

4

JAKE (*Turned on*)
Uh huh!
(*Strutting closer*)
Your prayers have been answered.

(MANNY *opens his eyes and for the first time looks at* JAKE)

MANNY
I don't want your money.

JAKE
I didn't offer any.

MANNY
I don't want anything from you.

JAKE
And that's what you'll get.

MANNY
You can't promise that. You don't know.

JAKE
I know what I'm willing to give.

MANNY
I know what I'm willing to give. But I can't promise.

JAKE
I can.

MANNY
Not for sure. You don't know.

5

JAKE

I know.

MANNY

Not for sure. And I need for sure.

(MANNY *returns to his praying position.* JAKE *stares in confusion.* HE *starts to leave again but stops*)

JAKE (*Belligerently*)

So, you wanna do it or what?

MANNY (*Opens his eyes. Quietly*)

Can you kiss?

JAKE (*Macho*)

I can't recall any complaints.

MANNY (*Suddenly an angry order*)

TALK!

JAKE (*Yelling back*)

What!?

MANNY

CAN. YOU. KISS?

JAKE (*Unsure*)

Yeah. Alright? Yeah, I can kiss.

MANNY (*Returning to prayer*)

Go away.

JAKE

What the hell's so important about kissing all of a sudden?

MANNY

Because you can't.

JAKE

Says you.

MANNY

I'm not giving you anything.

JAKE

I wouldn't take anything from you.

MANNY

You could take it. But you couldn't take it away. I need someone to take it away.

JAKE (*Frustrated*)

So, you wanna do it or what?

MANNY

Do I inspire you to lust?

JAKE

You fishing?

MANNY

Baiting.

JAKE (*Playing along sexily*)

What if I said yes?

7

MANNY

I'd have to say no.

JAKE

What do you want?

MANNY

What are you offering?

JAKE

A good time.

MANNY

That's all?

JAKE

What else do you want?

MANNY

Nothing.

JAKE

Great. You got it.

MANNY

You can't be sure.

JAKE

I'm sure, goddamnit!

MANNY (*Looking right at him*)

I meant what I said.

JAKE (*Challenging*)
Yeah? Well, me too.

MANNY
What'd you say?

JAKE (*"You first"*)
What'd you say?

MANNY
You can't kiss.

JAKE
Says you.
(JAKE *is fed up and starts to leave again*)

MANNY
I want you.

(JAKE *stops*)

MANNY
You're very beautiful.

(JAKE *turns back toward* MANNY)

MANNY
But I can't kiss.

(JAKE *has had his fill.* HE *starts to leave.* MANNY *faces forward, eyes open, and loudly recites.* JAKE *freezes in his path*)

9

MANNY

Two men meet in a bar and go home together. They have a drink, lower the lights, climb into bed, and they kiss.

Two grown men, mutually attracted, mutually in need, both of them hoping that this will be more than just another night.

Two grown men lie next to each other, facing each other, cheeks pressed flat to pillows, palms pressed to the mattress, knees firmly planted, thighs comfortably parted, rears raised high and waiting.

Two grown men wait next to each other equally willing, equally wanting, equally wishing to please. And they wait. Each waiting for the other to take. Each wanting only to give. And they wait. And they crumble. And they part. No one giving. No one getting. No one taking.

(*Pause, deep breath*)

Safe.

(*Pause*)

Safe.

(*Pause*)

Unhappy but safe.

(HE *smiles at* JAKE)

I wonder if you could understand how desperately I want to be with you.

JAKE

With me?

MANNY

No other.

JAKE

How far do you live?

MANNY

I've slept with thousands of men.

JAKE (*Getting excited*)

We'll go to my place.

MANNY

I can't go anywhere.

JAKE (*Trying to show the way*)

Come on.

MANNY

I can't see anyone.

JAKE

This way.

MANNY

I can't even kiss.

JAKE (*Suddenly realizing*)

Have you got it?

(MANNY *stares straight ahead*)

JAKE

Are you sick?

MANNY

What? No.

JAKE

No?

MANNY

No. You?

JAKE

Me? No. So? Let's go.

(JAKE *starts to lead on again but is stopped by* MAN-NY'*s recitation*)

MANNY (*loud and clear*)
Two grown men stand in a bar. Watching. Each other. They stare at each other. Each wanting the other. Two grown men stare in a bar, feet apart, eyes together, they stare. They sip. They puff. They want. Two grown men stare in a bar and then travel on in opposite directions. Never touching. Never holding. Never having. And why? Why? They can't kiss. They want to. They used to. They can't anymore.
(*Change of tone*)
A moment of silence for what we used to do and how it felt.

(JAKE *puts his hand to his heart out of respect.* MANNY *begins to weep quietly.* JAKE *stares.* MANNY'*s crying builds. Unsure what to do,* JAKE *reaches into his pocket and takes out a handkerchief [pink] and offers it to* MANNY. MANNY *stops and looks at the hanky*)

JAKE

It's alright. I washed it this morning. Hot water. And bleach.

(Thus assured, MANNY takes the hanky and uses it to blow his nose and wipe his eyes. HE reaches into his pocket and removes a small plastic bag. HE places the soiled hanky into the bag, seals the bag with a knot, and then hands it to JAKE)

MANNY

Thank you.

JAKE
(Putting it back in his pocket)
You're welcome.

MANNY

I feel better.

JAKE

I wasn't thinking.

MANNY

I was.

JAKE

Sometimes I forget.

MANNY

I try to.

JAKE

But you don't have it.

MANNY

No.

JAKE

And I don't have it.

MANNY

So?

JAKE (*Suggestively*)

So . . .

MANNY (*Begins to recite again*)

Two grown men stand in a bar looking at each other.
Four grown men stand in a bar looking at each other.
Eight grown men stand in a bar looking at each other.
Twelve grown men stand in a bar looking at each other.
Do they have it? Do they think? Do they forget? Can
they kiss?
Nine grown men stand in a bar looking at each other.
Five grown men stand in a bar looking at each other.
One grown man stands in a bar looking for someone
to look at.

(MANNY *turns and looks at* JAKE. JAKE *turns away
and leaves the stage.* MANNY *looks straight ahead.*
JAKE *returns to the stage dragging a life-size* dummy
of a man all dressed in lavender. HE *pulls it by its
arms to Center Stage and drops it at* MANNY's *feet.*
MANNY *looks down at the dummy.* JAKE *waits a beat,
and then exits again.*
JAKE *returns this time dragging a blue dummy after
him.* HE *dumps this one at* MANNY's *feet as well.*
MANNY *regards this dummy with an expressionless
stare.* JAKE *waits a beat and leaves again.*
JAKE *returns with a third* dummy, *this one dressed
in turquoise.*
As HE *drops this one onto the others . . .*)

MANNY
Don't drag your Ex's into this.

JAKE
They're yours.

(MANNY *takes a closer look at the dummies as* JAKE
exits again. HE *returns with a* yellow dummy)

MANNY
No more. Please.

(JAKE *adds this one to the pile and stands next to the
sofa.* MANNY *regards the dummies sadly*)

MANNY
I never wanted this. And I've always known what I
wanted. Done what I wanted. And never shunned the
responsibility of my actions. But not this. Not this.

JAKE
May I sit down?

MANNY (*Offering a seat*)
Please.

(JAKE *sits down next to* MANNY *and* THEY *stare together at the pile of dummies*)

MANNY
At fourteen years old I had a goal. A path. A vision all
my own. At fourteen years old I could see my destiny

so clearly that I could almost reach out with my bare hands and pull myself along the vortex of time. Impressed?

(JAKE *nods*)

MANNY

Want to know my goal?

JAKE

May I lie down?

MANNY (*Offering his lap*)

Please.

(JAKE *lies down and puts his head in* MANNY'S *lap*)

JAKE

Ready.

MANNY

My goal was to lie in the arms of every man. Every man.

JAKE (*Repeating*)

Every man.

MANNY

To lie in the arms of every man.

JAKE

Pet me.

(MANNY *looks at* JAKE *and smiles.* HE *begins to pet him gently.* JAKE *is soon purring like a kitten*)

MANNY

Every man.

JAKE (*Moaning*)

Every man.

MANNY

I never wanted anyone to wait. I never asked names. I offered a basic service; a barter, if you will. All up front. All explained. No small print. All understood. Your body for mine. Your moment for mine. Your knowledge, technique, history, scars . . . Your faults and shortcomings, your talents and abundances . . . No man too old. No face too deformed, weathered or nubile, ethnic or cliché . . . No form too bizarre; pumped up, stretched out, anorectic or bloated. Closet cases and radicals, perfect tens and amputees . . .

No advance too frivolous. No come-on waylaid. Want me? Take me. Be gentle. Be rough. Be generous. Be selfish. Go ahead; have a ball. Enjoy yourself. That's why I'm here. That's what I'm going to do.

JAKE (*Petted into ecstasy*)

Me too.

MANNY

Satisfaction was my aim. Mine and theirs. Separation was my only rule. My rule. I'm here now. Take. Be. Here. One minute. One hour. One day. Week. As long as the moment lasted. As long or as short as it took to end. But an end, even a pause, was the end. No pleading.

No excuses accepted. No arguments entertained. Understand and step aside. Say, "Thanks," and "Good-bye."

My goal: Every man. My rule. My law. No repeats. No attachments.

(*Looking down at the* dummies)

And I loved them all. And I missed them when they were gone. Done. Some more than others. And I was tempted to let them stay. Tempted to be tempted to stay. It would have been so easy so many times. So many Mr. Rights. So many comfortable beds. And lives. So many with so much to offer. Wealth, art, travel, danger . . . So much love, need, comfort . . .

And the good-byes. And the tears. And the smiles. Sweet morning kisses and rumpled sheets. Warm beds and spring breezes. Morning chills by spent fireplaces. Crisp cotton sheets in air-conditioned suites. Damp sleeping bags on forest leaves. Car seats. Theater balconies. Park benches. And coffee. Oh, the coffee. Coffee and good-byes . . . Off-to-work good-byes. Off-to-shop good-byes. Going home. Going on. Good-byes. So many lives. So many ways to live. So many men.

(MANNY *suddenly stops*)

JAKE

Don't stop.

MANNY

That's all.

JAKE

What about them?

MANNY

There are more.

JAKE

They look happy. Satisfied.

MANNY

That's funny. Do they?

JAKE

What about us?

MANNY

We're doing all we can.

JAKE

We have our problems.

MANNY

As to be expected.

JAKE

I want more.

MANNY
(*Reciting again and stops petting*)
Two grown men stand in a bar. They look. They touch.
They take. Two grown men forget. Want to forget.
And they go together. One gives. One gets. One gets
what the other does not intend to give. Doesn't even
know he's giving. Doesn't even know he had it to give.
Doesn't even have it himself. But can give. Two grown
men take. One gives. One gets. One weakens and dies.

(*Looking at the dummies*)
I didn't know.

JAKE
I believe you.

MANNY
I never wanted this.

JAKE
You have it.

MANNY
No, I give it. I give and give and give . . .

JAKE
What if I'm willing to take the risk?

MANNY
There's no risk. There's no question.

JAKE
You don't know.

MANNY
Ask them.

JAKE
But you didn't know then. Now you do.

MANNY
(*Returning to prayer position*)
Now I do. So, now I don't.

JAKE

There *are* ways around it. Things you can still do.

MANNY

Omissions.

JAKE

Precautions to take.

MANNY

Deletions.

JAKE

Alternate activities.

MANNY

Bastardizations.

JAKE

Positive, health-conscious acts of love and fulfillment.

MANNY (*Looking him in the eyes*)

Can you kiss?

(*This silences* JAKE, *who sits upright next to* MANNY)

MANNY

A moment of silence for what can't be done. Another for what can't be undone. A moment of silence for letting go of dreams. And one for stifled lives. For loss. For want. And a toast to those who can change. Who have changed. Who want to change and not forget.

JAKE

Come home with me.

(MANNY *looks at him and laughs ironically*)

JAKE

I'm not scared. I know what I'm doing.

MANNY

You don't know anything. One moment of passion,
one lapse of concentration, a second out of conscious-
ness, an instant of ecstasy and it's done.

JAKE

No one knows for sure.

MANNY

Doesn't matter. I'm done.

JAKE

We'll be careful.

MANNY

We can't kiss.

JAKE

I don't care.

MANNY (*Laughing again*)

I do!

JAKE

You shouldn't be alone.

MANNY

But I am.

JAKE

People shouldn't be alone.

MANNY

I'm not people anymore. I'm not even a disease. I'm a carrier of a disease. Another body in a hospital waiting room. Not a patient. Not a survivor. A fact. A statistic. No will. No dream. No choice.

(JAKE *stands and watches* MANNY *as* HE *begins to slip back into his prayer.* MANNY's *eyes slowly close and his hands begin to rise*)

JAKE

I'm sorry.

(MANNY *stops his progression and looks at* JAKE)

MANNY

Thank you.

JAKE

Well, I guess I'd better move on.

MANNY (*Sweetly*)

Good-bye.

JAKE

What are you going to do?

23

MANNY

I can't change. I can't. So, I'll sit. And remember. And pray for everything else to change. And when it does (and it will), I'll remember how to kiss.

(HE *smiles*)

And I will give only what I choose to give. What I mean to give. What I want to give. And I'll take only what I want from that which is offered. I will give and I will take without fear of small print or hidden clauses.

(*Quiet ecstasy*)

And I will kiss . . . ! I will kiss having learned nothing.

(MANNY's *smile freezes on his face as* HE *returns to silence.* JAKE *stares as the light fades away*)

THE END

SAFE
SEX

*

As the houselights dim we hear the crashing of waves on a beach. As the darkness grows so do the sounds. The waves are joined by the breathing and guttural whispers of TWO PEOPLE *making love. The sounds slowly become words.*

GHEE

Oh.

MEAD

Hah.

GHEE

Ho.

MEAD

Ah.

GHEE

No.

MEAD

Wha?

GHEE

No.

MEAD

Ya.

GHEE

Oh!

MEAD

Yeah.

GHEE

No!

MEAD

Why?

GHEE

Stop.

MEAD

No!

GHEE

No!

MEAD

Come on.

GHEE

You can't do that.

MEAD

It's alright.

GHEE

It's not.

MEAD

Don't stop.

GHEE

You can't do that.

MEAD

It's alright.

GHEE

It's not on the list.

MEAD

I need you.

GHEE

Check the list.

MEAD

Please.

GHEE

Where's the list?

MEAD

Don't.

GHEE

I'm checking the list.

MEAD

It's alright.

GHEE

Where's the light?

MEAD

Come on.

GHEE

I can't find the light.

MEAD

Come back here.

GHEE (*Yelling*)

It's not safe. Stop!

> (*The lights pop on brightly. The waves and all other sound ends abruptly as we stare at a bright white lit stage that is bare except for a giant fire-engine red seesaw [teeter-totter].*
> *As simply designed as possible, the balancing board has no handles; the base is triangular.*
> GHEE *and* MEAD *lie flat on the plank, facing up, their bare feet touching in the center, their heads at opposite ends.* THEY *are clothed in the sheerest of fabrics, the palest of pastels.*
> THEY *are perfectly balanced; the plank is perfectly horizontal.* THEY BOTH *pant, out of breath, from the struggle*)

GHEE
(*Slow and definite*)

Don't touch me.

(MEAD *does not move or react*)

GHEE

Did you hear what I said?

(*No reaction*)

GHEE

I'll get the list.

MEAD

Don't bother.

GHEE

I'm sure it wasn't safe.

MEAD

Sure.

GHEE

I'll show you right on the list.
(*Pause*)
You want to see it on the list?

MEAD

Forget it.

GHEE

'Cause you know I'm right and you know that if I show
it to you right on the list in black and white then you'll
have to admit that I'm right. Right?

MEAD

Right.

31

GHEE

You don't believe me. I'll get the list.

MEAD
(*Covering his face with his hands*)
Forget it. Just forget it. It doesn't matter. It's over.

(*Silence between them*)

GHEE

There aren't many things that I know a lot about, but on "Safe Sex" I happen to be an expert.

(*Another silence*)

GHEE

Did you say something?

MEAD

No.

GHEE

I hate when you get like this. Now you're mad at me when all I was trying to do was protect us both.

(*No response*)

GHEE

Why can't you stop when I ask you to? Huh?

(*No response*)

GHEE

Why does it always have to come to hurt feelings?

(GHEE *sits up straight.* HE *sees that* MEAD *is withdrawn.* HE *drops his head*)
I'm scared, alright? What's so hard to understand? I'm scared!

(*No response*)

GHEE

Being scared is smart. You have to be scared. You're supposed to be scared. You're not normal if you're not scared. Everyone's scared.

(*No response*)

GHEE

And I suppose you're not scared?

MEAD

I'm concerned.

GHEE

You're scared.

MEAD

I'm tired.

GHEE

You're angry.

MEAD

Don't tell me what I am.

GHEE

Don't yell at me.

33

MEAD

Don't tell me what to do.

GHEE

Don't touch me!

(THEY *turn their backs to each other, their legs hanging off the ends of the board. Balanced*)

GHEE

The honeymoon is over.
(*Pause*)
Would you say that was a safe assessment?

(*No response*)

GHEE

Lovers for five and a half years, separated for nearly two years, back together for less than a week and already the honeymoon is over.

MEAD (*Under his breath*)

Jerk.

GHEE

Fine. It's all my fault. Dump the blame on me. Like I don't feel guilty enough as is.

MEAD

I said you were a jerk. I wasn't blaming you for being a jerk. I didn't say that being a jerk was your fault. Nor was I attempting to make you feel guilty for being a jerk. I made a simple observation. You're a jerk. Now just drop it.

Harvey Fierstein in "Safe Sex"

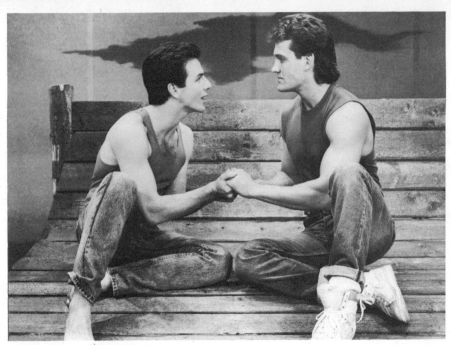

John Mulkeen and John Wesley Shipp in "Manny and Jake"

John Wesley Shipp and Harvey Fierstein in "Safe Sex"

Harvey Fierstein and Anne DeSalvo in "On Tidy Endings"

Harvey Fierstein, Ricky Addison Reed and Anne De Salvo in "On Tidy Endings"

GHEE

I'm a jerk because in the face of this devastating epidemic I insist we take a few precautions?

MEAD

No. You're just a jerk.

GHEE

Well, that's obvious. Who else but a jerk would want you back? Who else but a jerk would *take* you back? Who else but a jerk would fall in love with you in the first place?

MEAD

Want to see a list?

(GHEE *spins around and bounces on his end of the seesaw, throwing* MEAD *up into the air*)

MEAD

Damn!

(GHEE, *enjoying the advantage of having* MEAD *at his mercy, bounces the board for emphasis as* HE *speaks*)

GHEE

Well, come on. I'm waiting. Let's hear the list. How many?

MEAD

You know.

GHEE

No, you see, I only know about your little Larry. But

35

you said that there's a whole list. And much as you cared for him, I'd hardly call little Larry a list.

MEAD

You want to stop?

GHEE

I want to know how many. Larry and who else?

MEAD

Someone else.

GHEE

Who?

MEAD

You wouldn't know them.

GHEE

Them? How many of "them," Casanova?

MEAD

A few. Alright?

GHEE

Fine with me, but I wonder how little Larry felt about your "thems."

MEAD

Once I met Larry there was no one.

GHEE

No one?

MEAD

No one!
(MEAD *bounces hard on the board, tossing* GHEE *off
the ground, restoring the balance*)
He left me. I didn't leave him.

GHEE

And you came crawling back to me.

MEAD

You begged me to come back.

GHEE

I never begged!

MEAD

I never crawled!

(THEY *face off, staring each other down.* MEAD *breaks
it*)

MEAD

I hate when you do this! You're not happy unless you've
got me bashing your head into a wall.

(GHEE *lies back glamorously*)

GHEE

I'm horny.

(*No response*)

GHEE

There's definitely something wrong with me. All I have

37

to do is think about you with someone else and I get crazy. What's that: love?

MEAD

Jealousy.

GHEE

No. You think? No! Well . . . Yeah. Maybe. But if that's jealousy why does everyone put it down?

MEAD

It's an immature emotion. As irrational as it is insulting. It puts an object value on pure emotion and reduces what should be a free partnership into possessor and possessed.

GHEE

I love it.
(*Pause*)
Whenever I remember your first telling me that you had slept with someone else, all I can think about is the incredible sex we had that night.
(*Giggles*)
I don't remember pain, though I know there was. I don't remember anger, though there certainly was some of that. Just this overwhelming burning that flamed into the most intense passion I had ever felt.
(*Pause*)
Remember?

MEAD

I remember waiting for you to scream. Guilt. I remember waiting to be punished. Hurt. I remember lying next to you after you'd fallen asleep and thinking about the sex we had just had.

GHEE

It was great, wasn't it?

MEAD

Could have been. That wasn't important. All I remember is that that was the first time you had touched me, let alone made love to me, in over three months.

GHEE (*Angry*)

That's a lie.

MEAD

True.

GHEE
(*Bolting up to look at him*)

It wasn't three months.

(MEAD *stares* GHEE *down*)

GHEE

Maybe three days. Or maybe three weeks.

(MEAD *just stares.* GHEE *submits.* THEY BOTH *lie back once again. Silence. Balance*)

GHEE

I was scared.
(*Pause*)

It was a bad time for me. All you read about, every headline, the only thing on TV, was AIDS. Joey had already died. Tommy was in the hospital. And how many other friends did we have who had it? How many others did we think might?

MEAD

So, I got locked out.

GHEE

I was scared.

MEAD

Of what? We'd been together for five years. We'd already done everything they said you shouldn't. If one of us did have it, if one of us was going to infect the other, it was already done.

GHEE

I was in a panic. I wasn't thinking.

MEAD

You were thinking. About yourself.

GHEE

And you. Before we met I was pretty wild. You talk about your lists? Boy if I had to, I don't think I could ever remember all the guys I had sex with.

MEAD

You didn't have sex with anyone. Trust me, I laid next to you all those years. Sex is something you don't have. Oh, you fiddle and diddle, but sex? Real sex?

GHEE

I don't remember getting any complaints.

MEAD

You never hung around long enough to hear them.

GHEE

That's bull.

MEAD

Think so?

GHEE

What about us our first year? We never got out of bed.

MEAD

I don't remember.

GHEE

You couldn't keep your hands off me.

MEAD

That so?

GHEE

I used to have to beg for dinner breaks.

MEAD

That was years ago.

GHEE

Years before AIDS.

MEAD

Our problems started years before AIDS. AIDS was your salvation.

GHEE

That's sick.

MEAD

You ran right out, got your list of Do's and Don'ts and embraced it like a priest takes his vows. Safe Sex, there in black and white you finally had what you always wanted: a concrete, board-certified, actual, purposeful excuse to avoid intimacy. God, you were in your glory! You waved it in my face with one hand and shoved me across the bed with the other. You took your list and nailed it to the headboard like the goddamned sexual commandments: "Thou shalt not . . . Thou shalt not . . . Thou shalt not . . ." You're not scared of AIDS, you're scared of sex.

GHEE

Me?

MEAD

Or me.

GHEE

You're scared of sex?

MEAD

You're scared of me.

GHEE

Me scared of you? Don't flatter yourself.

MEAD

When I first started fooling around I reasoned that I was justified. I certainly wasn't getting anything at home. I had a right to look elsewhere. But my lies were so blatant, my excuses so lame . . . I wanted you to catch me. I wanted you to know that you could lose, actually lose, me. I did it right under your nose, right in your bed . . . I left phone numbers around, and clothing . . . And nothing!

GHEE

I suspected.

MEAD

You hoped. Wished even. One more excuse to push me away.

GHEE

And what were you doing? Your fooling around was supposed to make me feel safer? What are you, out of your mind?

MEAD

Didn't it? You just said that the best sex we ever had was after you found out about Larry. When there actually was danger. When I actually could have been infected.

GHEE

That was different. We had Safe Sex.

MEAD

We had Safe Distance, and that's all you've ever wanted.

(*Silence.* BOTH *consider what has been said.* GHEE *sits up, cross-legged, and looks at* MEAD)

43

GHEE

So what're you saying; that I'm a lousy lay?

(MEAD *covers his head in frustration*)

GHEE

That your complaint, dearie? That you got stuck with a lukewarm lover? Well, fill your ears with this, buddy: I've got two faucets, hot and cold, and if you were getting lukewarm loving then maybe it's because that's what you dialed.

MEAD

Fine. It's all my fault.

GHEE

Hey, don't try and shut me off. You ran this shower, now stand under it.
(*Deep breath*)
So, you laid alone in bed, did ya? You were forced to walk the streets for affection, eh? Let me tell you something, Samantha, you could have had all the sex you wanted. You could've had intimacy pouring out your eyeballs. All you had to do was wash up.

MEAD

Cheese and crackers!

GHEE

Shut up! You had your chance to mouth your neo-Nietzsche nonsense, now it's my turn at bat.

(GHEE *and* MEAD *now sit up fully, legs dangling from the board.* THEY *balance*)

GHEE

You'd come home to me night after night all hot and sweaty from a hard day's work. You'd drift through the door after stopping for a few brews with the boys, reeking of beer, clothes soaked through, hair as greasy as a used-up peanut butter jar, and you'd throw your arms out to me and say, "Baby, I need your lovin'," and expect me to swoon. I swooned alright!

(MEAD *opens his mouth to protest*)

GHEE

I said shut up!

(MEAD *shakes his head and remains silent*)

GHEE

Now, I will admit to finding the air pretty sexy for the first year. It was like living in a John Garfield fantasy, my very own hot blue-collared lover leaving armpit stains on my settee; but after a year? But I figured it was a stage, a phase. After all, when we were first dating you'd show up perfectly coiffed and cologned, and it was a chore and challenge to melt you down. But here we were, fairly crossing the threshold, and I'd traded my Arthurian knight in for his white horse.

I will grant you, there are those with penchants for farm follies. I do not, however, happen to march in their number. And I'd say, "Baby, wouldn't you like to clean up first?"

And you'd say, "No."

And I'd say, "Darling, how about we take a shower together?"

And you'd say, "How 'bout we don't?" and laugh a laugh as soiled as your sweat socks.

MEAD

Have you no shame?

GHEE

My sex and sensuality have been attacked. There's no time for illusions. You'd strip down and crawl all fil-thified into my beautiful crisp clean bed and lie there with a beer in one hand, the remote control in the other, watching some ball game or other . . .

MEAD
(*Pushing off the ground with his feet*)
I was waiting for you to come to bed, but you were always off somewhere messing around with who knows what.

GHEE
(*Pushing off with his feet as well*)
I was throwing in a wash. I was scared what would happen if I left your clothes in the hamper overnight.

(*Now, with each countering point,* GHEE *and* MEAD *push the ground with their feet so that* THEY *are soon seesawing like mad*)

MEAD

You really stink.

GHEE

I? I!?!?! Now let's talk about your feet. I've seen dogs

fall in love with spots of grass where you'd walked barefoot.

MEAD

Now I've heard everything.

GHEE

Not by a long shot.

MEAD

I showered every morning.

GHEE

You'd never know it at night.

MEAD

If I wash my hair at night it stands up funny in the morning.

GHEE

Wash it again.

MEAD

I'd be bald!

GHEE

You'd be happy!

MEAD

You'd be happy!

GHEE

And that's bad? You knew how I felt. I told you often enough.

47

MEAD

You never told me, you nagged.

GHEE

So, you knew. You couldn't make the effort.

MEAD

You're still avoiding the real issue.

GHEE

What's the real issue? That I pushed you away?

MEAD

That you couldn't be with me.

GHEE

I couldn't *breathe* with you.

MEAD

You're impossible!

GHEE

God, I feel great!
(GHEE *begins to laugh with excitement*)
It feels so good to finally get that said.

(MEAD *stops the seesaw abruptly. His feet on the
ground,* HE *has* GHEE *in his power, up in the air.*
THEY *face off again, only now it is with sexual excitement*)

MEAD

You love the way I smell.

48

GHEE (*Taunting him*)
That so?

MEAD
You missed me when I wasn't there.

GHEE
Says you.

MEAD
When I'd stay out all night I'd come home and find you in bed with one of my jackets or shirts.

GHEE (*Lying back sexily*)
Maybe I was cold.

(MEAD *begins to bounce the board gently, sensuously*)

MEAD
Maybe you was gettin' hot. You always smelled of soap. You showered in the morning, showered before bed, showered after sex . . .

GHEE
I was just trying to keep your stink offa me. I was bathing for two.
(HE *begins to giggle*)

MEAD
What? Come on, what?

GHEE
Ever notice how pruney my skin was?

MEAD

No. It was soft.

GHEE

My fingertips always looked like something you'd pull out of a box of health-food cereal.

(GHEE *begins to slowly slide down the board toward* MEAD. MEAD *continues to pump the board*)

MEAD

Your skin was always cool and lightly moist. I remember powder.

GHEE

I use cornstarch.

MEAD

Silky.

GHEE

Smoother.

MEAD

I'd nustle up against you.

GHEE

Your hands were always dry and rough.

MEAD

I'd pull as close against you as I could.

GHEE

I'd turn my head into the pillow.

MEAD
I couldn't get close enough.

GHEE
I couldn't get far enough away.

MEAD
I rubbed against your back.

GHEE
I'd pull the covers over my head.

MEAD
I kissed your neck.

GHEE
I bit the pillow.

(GHEE *is almost in his arms.* MEAD *reaches out*)

MEAD
I wanted you so badly.

GHEE
(*Suddenly jumping up and yelling*)
Not bad enough to wash!

MEAD
Alright, you win! Let's wash!

GHEE
Now?

MEAD

Together.

GHEE

You mean it?

MEAD

I mean it.

GHEE

I love you.

MEAD (*Arms around him*)

Let's go.

GHEE (*Stopping everything*)

But is it safe? I'd better check the list.

(MEAD *lies straight back in acute frustration and moans*)

GHEE

What's the big deal? It'll take me two seconds and this way we can be sure.

(MEAD *simply moans, shaking his head and covering his face with his arms*)

MEAD

No. No. No. No . . .

GHEE

On second thought I'm sure it's safe. No, it's safe. In fact I'm positive it's safe. As a matter of record it is not only safe *but* I believe it is highly recommended. It is, as I now recall, the very first rule on the list. The very cornerstone on which Safe Sex is built. So, let's go for it!

(GHEE *starts to move.* MEAD *does not*)

GHEE
Okay? Let's go!

(*No movement*)

GHEE
Alright, we're moving now!

(GHEE *starts to move.* MEAD *remains still*)

GHEE
Okay. GO!!!

(*Still* MEAD *remains.* GHEE *looks at him unhappily.*
HE *reaches out and lifts one of* MEAD's *legs.* HE *lets go of it and it drops lifelessly.*
GHEE *backs away from* MEAD *and begins to rock the board gently as you would a carriage*)

GHEE
You okay?
(*A pause*)
I did this, didn't I?

(*No response*)

GHEE
Whatever happened to sex being fun?

53

Whatever happened to sex being dirty?
Whatever happened to sex being something we did?
(*Studies* MEAD)
I hope you don't think that I was trying to insult you
before. Because I wasn't. Are you insulted?

MEAD

Frustrated.

GHEE

But not insulted.

MEAD

No.

GHEE

Good.
(HE *lies down flat on his back. Pause*)
You wanna play Yahtzee?

MEAD

No.

GHEE

C'mon. Let's play a game. How about Monopoly?

MEAD

No.

GHEE

Scrabble?

MEAD

No.

GHEE

Risk!

(MEAD *jumps with excitement.* GHEE *quickly pulls away*)

GHEE

No! I don't want to play Risk.

(MEAD *lies back down in frustration.* GHEE *thinks*)

GHEE

Can I tell you how I felt about you when we first met? How I felt about us?

MEAD

Be my guest.

GHEE

You won't be insulted.

MEAD

No. Probably just frustrated.

GHEE

Good.

(Fresh start)

You know that you were my first love. My only love. Except if you count you then and you now. But then you'd have to count me then and me now, so I guess "only" still goes.

You was a baby. I was all growed up. You practically lost your virginity. I'd practically lost count.

I tiptoed through your life, living on the edges, covering my tracks, remaining secret and quiet, and was quite happy. They were different times.

Is it enough to say that they were different times? I mean, I had a life, you had a life and we had a life. I lived in my world, you lived in your world and then we shared a bed. We had great sex, but argued politics: to be or not to be in the closet, separatism, legalization, legislation . . . Politics were argued, sex was great. Different times.

I believe there were fewer Nautilus machines then. There certainly were fewer gyms. We were certainly happier with ourselves. And we loved each other. We shared what we could when we could and our fear was of them that would not let us be. Our anger was for them that would not let us be. Our comfort was being with each other.

Not so different. But different enough.

When I picture you then, I see a man prone in my bed and waiting. No expectations or demands. Just a man, waiting to be with another man, where he was happy and belonged. A nervous smile, an unassumed pose, patient, excited, warm and delicious.

And we were together without question. There at that moment, in the present, together. Perfectly balanced: need and satisfaction. Evenly matched. We soared. And sex was unimportant like air and water.

We had no lists of Do's and Don'ts. There was no death count. The worst you could get from loving was a broken heart. Which you gave me! And I lived. Remember herpes? Remember crabs? Remember worrying about the clap?

And we were invisible. Nobody knew who we were for sure. We were the great chic mysterious underground and I loved every minute!

And then came now.

Different times. Now we enjoy politics and argue sex. Now they know who we are. We're counted in their surveys. We're numbered in their watchfulness. We're powered in their press. We're courted, polled, placated . . . The myths slowly peel away and the mysteries fade. Now they know that we're teachers and doctors and lawyers and priests and mothers and babies. Now they see us everywhere: hospitals, classrooms, theaters, obituaries . . . Now when they tell lies about us we answer back. We've found our voices. We know who we are. They know who we are. And they know that we care what they think.

And all because of a disease. A virus. A virus that you don't get because you're Gay, just because you're human. We were Gay. Now we're human.

Y'know, if anyone had ever tried to tell me that one day I would push you across the bed . . . But I did. I did because it wasn't safe for one person to love another person as much as I loved you. And that was *then*!

> (*Fondly looking at* MEAD; *it is as if* THEY *were renewing their wedding vows*)

Now? I love you more now than I did on our most carefree day. I trust you more now than before you renounced our commitment. I need you more now than when you were away from me. I want you more now . . .

And it's impossible. Even if you fought me and won. Even if you broke through and got me to admit who you truly are to me . . .

We can never touch as before. We can never be as before.

"Now" will always define us. Different times. Too late.
>   (*The anger builds inside of him*)
At last we have Safe Sex.

>   GHEE
>   (*Turning accusingly to the audience*)
Safe for them!
>   (*Pulling back into himself*)
I'm angry.
I'm frightened.
I'm alone.

>   MEAD
You're not alone.

>   GHEE
I feel alone.

> (MEAD *jumps to his feet and stands on the very end of his side of the board*)

>   MEAD
Well, you're not.

>   GHEE
>   (*Clutching the board for safety*)
What're you doing?

>   MEAD
I love you.

>   GHEE
I love you too, now sit down.

58

MEAD (*Motioning*)

Come on then, get up.

GHEE

You're out of your mind.

MEAD

After five years with you, who wouldn't be. Get up.

GHEE

You're going to kill yourself.

MEAD

What're you, scared?

GHEE

It's not safe.

MEAD

Then check your list first and then get up.

GHEE

For this I don't have to check no list.

MEAD

Then come on.

GHEE

No.

MEAD

You want to be alone the rest of your life? I came back
once. Want to bet if I come back again?

GHEE (*Starting to stand*)
Can't we shower first?

MEAD
Later. Come on, you're doing great.

GHEE (*Almost standing*)
I'm scared.

MEAD
This is dangerous. You're supposed to be.

(GHEE *stands up fully and the board balances once again.* THEY *stand at opposite ends, facing each other.* GHEE *is frightened,* MEAD *is proud of him*)

MEAD
These are different times with different rules, but some things never change.

GHEE
What are you talking about?

MEAD
Do you trust me?

GHEE
Yes. Can I get down now?

MEAD
Do you believe in me?

GHEE
I told you I did.

MEAD
And you believe I love you?

GHEE
Whatever you say.

(MEAD *stares*)

GHEE
Alright. Yes.

(MEAD *takes a step toward* GHEE. *The board remains perfectly balanced.* GHEE *is terrified*)

MEAD
Do you believe in miracles?

GHEE
I don't know. I guess so.

(MEAD *takes another step toward* GHEE. GHEE *waves his arms wildly to keep balance but there's no need, the board remains perfectly balanced*)

GHEE
I love when you take charge.

(MEAD *takes another step toward* GHEE. GHEE *begins to relax*)

MEAD
I love you.

(MEAD *walks to the exact center of the board.* GHEE
remains still, hanging in space)

GHEE

I love you too.

MEAD

That's all that matters.

(MEAD *holds out his hands to have* GHEE *join him in
the center.* GHEE *walks toward him*)

MEAD

The rest is a piece of cake.

GHEE (*Reaching him*)

Promise?

MEAD (*Arms around* GHEE)

Promise.

GHEE (*Melting in the embrace*)

Let's shower.

(*Blackout*)

THE END

ON
TIDY
ENDINGS

*

The curtain rises on a deserted, modern Upper West Side apartment. In the bright daylight that pours in through the windows we can see the living room of the apartment. Far Stage Right is the galley kitchen, next to it the multilocked front door with intercom. Stage Left reveals a hallway that leads to the two bedrooms and baths.

Though the room is still fully furnished (couch, coffee table, etc.), there are boxes stacked against the wall and several photographs and paintings are on the floor leaving shadows on the wall where they once hung. Obviously someone is moving out. From the way the boxes are neatly labeled and stacked, we know that this is an organized person.

From the hallway just outside the door we hear the rattling of keys and two arguing voices:

JIM (*Offstage*)
I've got to be home by four. I've got practice.

MARION (*Offstage*)
I'll get you to practice, don't worry.

JIM (*Offstage*)
I don't want to go in there.

MARION (*Offstage*)

Jimmy, don't make Mommy crazy, alright? We'll go inside, I'll call Aunt Helen and see if you can go down and play with Robbie.

(*The door opens.*
MARION *is a handsome woman of forty. Dressed in a business suit, her hair conservatively combed,* SHE *appears to be going to a business meeting.*
JIM *is a boy of eleven. His playclothes are typical, but someone has obviously just combed his hair.*
MARION *recovers the key from the lock*)

JIM

Why can't I just go down and ring the bell?

MARION

Because I said so.

(*As* MARION *steps into the room* SHE *is a struck by some unexpected emotion.* SHE *freezes in her path and stares at the empty apartment.* JIM *lingers by the door*)

JIM

I'm going downstairs.

MARION

Jimmy, please.

JIM

This place gives me the creeps.

MARION

This was your father's apartment. There's nothing creepy about it.

JIM

Says you.

MARION

You want to close the door, please?

(JIM *reluctantly obeys*)

MARION

Now, why don't you go check your room and make sure you didn't leave anything.

JIM

It's empty.

MARION

Go look.

JIM

I looked last time.

MARION (*Trying to be patient*)

Honey, we sold the apartment. You're never going to be here again. Go make sure you have everything you want.

JIM

But Uncle Arthur packed everything.

MARION (*Less patiently*)

Go make sure.

JIM

There's nothing in there.

MARION (*Exploding*)

I said make sure!

(JIM *jumps, then realizing that* SHE's *not kidding, obeys*)

MARION

Everything's an argument with that one.
(SHE *looks around the room and breathes deeply. There is sadness here. Under her breath:*)
I can still smell you.
(*Suddenly not wanting to be alone*)
Jimmy? Are you okay?

JIM (*Returning*)

Nothing. Told you so.

MARION

Uncle Arthur must have worked very hard. Make sure you thank him.

JIM

What for? Robbie says,
(*Fey mannerisms*)
"They love to clean up things!"

MARION

Sometimes you can be a real joy.

JIM

Did you call Aunt Helen?

MARION

Do I get a break here?
(*Approaching the* BOY *understandingly*)
Wouldn't you like to say good-bye?

JIM

To who?

MARION

To the apartment. You and your daddy spent a lot of
time here together. Don't you want to take one last look
around?

JIM

Ma, get a real life.

MARION

"Get a real life."
(*Going for the phone*)
Nice. Very nice.

JIM

Could you call already?

MARION (*Dialing*)
Jimmy, what does this look like I'm doing?

(JIM *kicks at the floor impatiently. Someone answers
the phone at the other end*)

MARION
(*Into the phone*)
Helen? Hi, we're upstairs. . . . No, we just walked in

the door. Jimmy wants to know if he can come down. . . . Oh, thanks.

(*Hearing that,* JIM *breaks for the door*)

MARION
(*Yelling after him*)
Don't run in the halls! And don't play with the elevator buttons!

(*The door slams shut behind him*)

MARION
(*Back to the phone*)
Hi. . . . No, I'm okay. It's a little weird being here. . . . No. Not since the funeral, and then there were so many people. Jimmy told me to get "a real life." I don't think I could handle anything realer. . . . No, please. Stay where you are. I'm fine. The doorman said Arthur would be right back and my lawyer should have been here already. . . . Well, we've got the papers to sign and a few other odds and ends to clean up. Shouldn't take long.

(*The intercom buzzer rings*)

MARION
Hang on, that must be her.
(MARION *goes to the intercom and speaks*)
Yes? . . . Thank you.
(*Back to the phone*)
Helen? Yeah, it's the lawyer. I'd better go. . . . Well, I could use a stiff drink, but I drove down. Listen, I'll stop by on my way out. Okay? Okay. 'Bye.

(SHE *hangs up the phone, looks around the room. That uncomfortable feeling returns to her quickly.* SHE *gets up and goes to the front door, opens it and looks out. No one there yet.* SHE *closes the door, shakes her head knowing that* SHE*'s being silly and starts back into the room.* SHE *looks around, can't make it and retreats to the door.* SHE *opens it, looks out, closes it, but stays right there, her hand on the doorknob. The bell rings.* SHE *throws open the door)*

MARION

That was quick.

(JUNE LOWELL *still has her finger on the bell. Her arms are loaded with contracts.* MARION*'s contemporary,* JUNE *is less formal in appearance and more hyper in her manner)*

JUNE

That was quicker. What, were you waiting by the door?

MARION (*Embarrassed*)

No. I was just passing it. Come on in.

JUNE

Have you got your notary seal?

MARION

I think so.

JUNE

Great. Then you can witness. I left mine at the office and thanks to gentrification I'm double-parked downstairs.

(*Looking for a place to dump her load*)
Where?

MARION
(*Definitely pointing to the coffee table*)
Anywhere. You mean you're not staying?

JUNE
If you really think you need me I can go down and find
a parking lot. I think there's one over on Columbus.
So, I can go down, park the car in the lot and take a
cab back if you really think you need me.

MARION
Well . . . ?

JUNE
But you shouldn't have any problems. The papers are
about as straightforward as papers get. Arthur is giving
you power of attorney to sell the apartment and you're
giving him a check for half the purchase price. Everything else is just signing papers that state that you know
that you signed the other papers. Anyway, he knows
the deal, his lawyers have been over it all with him, it's
just a matter of signatures.

MARION (*Not fine*)
Oh, fine.

JUNE
Unless you just don't want to be alone with him . . . ?

MARION
With Arthur? Don't be silly.

JUNE (*Laying out the papers*)
Then you'll handle it solo? Great. My car thanks you, the parking lot thanks you, and the cab driver that wouldn't have gotten a tip thanks you. Come have a quick look-see.

MARION (*Joining her on the couch*)
There are a lot of papers here.

JUNE
Copies. Not to worry. Start here.

(MARION *starts to read*)

JUNE
I ran into Jimmy playing Elevator Operator.

(MARION *jumps*)

JUNE
I got him off at the sixth floor. Read on.

MARION
This is definitely not my day for dealing with him.

(JUNE *gets up and has a look around*)

JUNE
I don't believe what's happening to this neighborhood. You made quite an investment when you bought this place.

MARION
Collin was always very good at figuring out those things.

73

JUNE

Well, he sure figured this place right. What, have you tripled your money in ten years?

MARION

More.

JUNE

It's a shame to let it go.

MARION

We're not ready to be a two-dwelling family.

JUNE

So, sublet it again.

MARION

Arthur needs the money from the sale.

JUNE

Arthur got plenty already. I'm not crying for Arthur.

MARION

I don't hear you starting in again, do I?

JUNE

Your interests and your wishes are my only concern.

MARION

Fine.

JUNE

I still say we should contest Collin's will.

MARION

June . . . !

JUNE

You've got a child to support.

MARION

And a great job, and a husband with a great job. Tell me what Arthur's got.

JUNE

To my thinking, half of everything that should have gone to you. And more. All of Collin's personal effects, his record collection . . .

MARION

And I suppose their three years together meant nothing.

JUNE

When you compare them to your sixteen-year marriage? Not nothing, but not half of everything.

MARION
(*Trying to change the subject*)
June, who gets which copies?

JUNE

Two of each to Arthur. One you keep. The originals and anything else come back to me.
(*Looking around*)
I still say you should've sublet the apartment for a year and then sold it. You would've gotten an even better price. Who wants to buy an apartment when they know someone died in it. No one. And certainly no one wants

75

to buy an apartment when they know the person died of AIDS.

MARION (*Snapping*)
June. Enough!

JUNE (*Catching herself*)
Sorry. That was out of line. Sometimes my mouth does that to me. Hey, that's why I'm a lawyer. If my brain worked as fast as my mouth I would have gotten a real job.

MARION (*Holding out a stray paper*)
What's this?

JUNE
I forgot. Arthur's lawyer sent that over yesterday. He found it in Collin's safety-deposit box. It's an insurance policy that came along with some consulting job he did in Japan. He either forgot about it when he made out his will or else he wanted you to get the full payment. Either way, it's yours.

MARION
Are you sure we don't split this?

JUNE
Positive.

MARION
But everything else . . . ?

JUNE
Hey, Arthur found it, his lawyer sent it to me. Relax,

it's all yours. Minus my commission, of course. Go out and buy yourself something. Anything else before I have to use my cut to pay the towing bill?

MARION

I guess not.

JUNE (*Starting to leave*)
Great. Call me when you get home.
(*Stopping at the door and looking back*)
Look, I know that I'm attacking this a little coldly. I am aware that someone you loved has just died. But there's a time and place for everything. This is about tidying up loose ends, not holding hands. I hope you'll remember that when Arthur gets here. Call me.

(*And* SHE's *gone*)
(MARION *looks ill at ease to be alone again.* SHE *nervously straightens the papers into neat little piles, looks at them and then remembers:*)

MARION

Pens. We're going to need pens.

(*At last a chore to be done.* SHE *looks in her purse and finds only one.* SHE *goes to the kitchen and opens a drawer where* SHE *finds two more.* SHE *starts back to the table with them but suddenly remembers something else.* SHE *returns to the kitchen and begins going through the cabinets until* SHE *finds what* SHE's *looking for: a blue Art Deco teapot. Excited to find it,* SHE *takes it back to the couch.*
Guilt strikes. SHE *stops, considers putting it back, wavers, then:*)

MARION
(*To herself*)
Oh, he won't care. One less thing to pack.

(SHE *takes the teapot and places it on the couch next
to her purse.* SHE *is happier. Now* SHE *searches the
room with her eyes for any other treasures* SHE *may
have overlooked. Nothing here.* SHE *wanders off into
the bedroom.*
We hear keys outside the front door. ARTHUR *lets
himself into the apartment carrying a load of empty
cartons and a large shopping bag.*
ARTHUR *is in his mid-thirties, pleasant looking though
sloppily dressed in work clothes and slightly over-
weight.*
ARTHUR *enters the apartment just as* MARION *comes
out of the bedroom carrying a framed watercolor painting.* THEY *jump at the sight of each other*)

MARION
Oh, hi, Arthur. I didn't hear the door.

ARTHUR (*Staring at the painting*)
Well hello, Marion.

MARION (*Guiltily*)
I was going to ask you if you were thinking of taking
this painting because if you're not going to then I'll take
it. Unless, of course, you want it.

ARTHUR
No. You can have it.

MARION

I never really liked it, actually. I hate cats. I didn't even like the show. I needed something for my college dorm room. I was never the rock star poster type. I kept it in the back of a closet for years until Collin moved in here and took it. He said he liked it.

ARTHUR

I do too.

MARION

Well, then you keep it.

ARTHUR

No. Take it.

MARION

We've really got no room for it. You keep it.

ARTHUR

I don't want it.

MARION

Well, if you're sure.

ARTHUR (*Seeing the teapot*)

You want the teapot?

MARION

If you don't mind.

ARTHUR

One less thing to pack.

79

MARION

Funny, but that's exactly what I thought. One less thing to pack. You know, my mother gave it to Collin and me when we moved in to our first apartment. Silly sentimental piece of junk, but you know.

ARTHUR

That's not the one.

MARION

Sure it is. Hall used to make them for Westinghouse back in the thirties. I see them all the time at antiques shows and I always wanted to buy another, but they ask such a fortune for them.

ARTHUR

We broke the one your mother gave you a couple of years ago. That's a reproduction. You can get them almost anywhere in the Village for eighteen bucks.

MARION

Really? I'll have to pick one up.

ARTHUR

Take this one. I'll get another.

MARION

No, it's yours. You bought it.

ARTHUR

One less thing to pack.

MARION

Don't be silly. I didn't come here to raid the place.

ARTHUR

Well, was there anything else of Collin's that you thought you might like to have?

MARION

Now I feel so stupid, but actually I made a list. Not for me. But I started thinking about different people; friends, relatives, you know, that might want to have something of Collin's to remember him by. I wasn't sure just what you were taking and what you were throwing out. Anyway, I brought the list.
(*Gets it from her purse*)
Of course these are only suggestions. You probably thought of a few of these people yourself. But I figured it couldn't hurt to write it all down. Like I said, I don't know what you are planning on keeping.

ARTHUR (*Taking the list*)

I was planning on keeping it all.

MARION

Oh, I know. But most of these things are silly. Like his high school yearbooks. What would you want with them?

ARTHUR

Sure. I'm only interested in his Gay period.

MARION

I didn't mean it that way. Anyway, you look it over. They're only suggestions. Whatever you decide to do is fine with me.

ARTHUR (*Folding the list*)

It would have to be, wouldn't it. I mean, it's all mine now. He did leave this all to me.

81

(MARION *is becoming increasingly nervous, but tries
to keep a light approach as* SHE *takes a small bundle
of papers from her bag*)

MARION

While we're on the subject of what's yours. I brought
a batch of condolence cards that were sent to you care
of me. Relatives mostly.

ARTHUR (*Taking them*)

More cards? I'm going to have to have another printing
of thank-you notes done.

MARION

I answered these last week, so you don't have to bother.
Unless you want to.

ARTHUR

Forge my signature?

MARION

Of course not. They were addressed to both of us and
they're mostly distant relatives or friends we haven't
seen in years. No one important.

ARTHUR

If they've got my name on them, then I'll answer them
myself.

MARION

I wasn't telling you not to, I was only saying that you
don't have to.

ARTHUR

I understand.

(MARION *picks up the teapot and brings it to the kitchen*)

MARION

Let me put this back.

ARTHUR

I ran into Jimmy in the lobby.

MARION

Tell me you're joking.

ARTHUR

I got him to Helen's.

MARION

He's really racking up the points today.

ARTHUR

You know, he still can't look me in the face.

MARION

He's reacting to all of this in strange ways. Give him time. He'll come around. He's really very fond of you.

ARTHUR

I know. But he's at that awkward age: under thirty. I'm sure in twenty years we'll be the best of friends.

MARION

It's not what you think.

ARTHUR

What do you mean?

MARION

Well, you know.

ARTHUR

No I don't know. Tell me.

MARION

I thought that you were intimating something about his blaming you for Collin's illness and I was just letting you know that it's not true.
(*Foot in mouth,* SHE *braves on*)
We discussed it a lot and . . . uh . . . he understands that his father was sick before you two ever met.

ARTHUR

I don't believe this.

MARION

I'm just trying to say that he doesn't blame you.

ARTHUR

First of all, who asked you? Second of all, that's between him and me. And third and most importantly, of course he blames me. Marion, he's eleven years old. You can discuss all you want, but the fact is that his father died of a "fag" disease and I'm the only fag around to finger.

MARION

My son doesn't use that kind of language.

ARTHUR

Forget the language. I'm talking about what he's been through. Can you imagine the kind of crap he's taken from his friends? That poor kid's been chased and chastised from one end of town to the other. He's got to have someone to blame just to survive. He can't blame you, you're all he's got. He can't blame his father; he's dead. So, Uncle Arthur gets the shaft. Fine, I can handle it.

MARION

You are so wrong, Arthur. I know my son and that is not the way his mind works.

ARTHUR

I don't know what you know. I only know what I know. And all I know is what I hear and see. The snide remarks, the little smirks . . . And it's not just the illness. He's been looking for a scapegoat since the day you and Collin first split up. Finally he has one.

MARION (*Getting very angry now*)

Wait. Are you saying that if he's going to blame someone it should be me?

ARTHUR

I think you should try to see things from his point of view.

MARION

Where do you get off thinking you're privy to my son's point of view?

ARTHUR

It's not that hard to imagine. Life's rolling right along, he's having a happy little childhood, when suddenly one day his father's moving out. No explanations, no reasons, none of the fights that usually accompany such things. Divorce is hard enough for a kid to understand when he's listened to years of battles, but yours?

MARION

So what should we have done? Faked a few months' worth of fights before Collin moved out?

ARTHUR

You could have told him the truth, plain and simple.

MARION

He was seven years old at the time. How the hell do you tell a seven-year-old that his father is leaving his mother to go sleep with other men?

ARTHUR

Well, not like that.

MARION

You know, Arthur, I'm going to say this as nicely as I can: Butt out. You're not his mother and you're not his father.

ARTHUR

Thank you. I wasn't acutely aware of that fact. I will certainly keep that in mind from now on.

MARION

There's only so much information a child that age can handle.

ARTHUR

So it's best that he reach his capacity on the street.

MARION

He knew about the two of you. We talked about it.

ARTHUR

Believe me, he knew before you talked about it. He's young, not stupid.

MARION

It's very easy for you to stand here and criticize, but there are aspects that you will just never be able to understand. You weren't there. You have no idea what it was like for me. You're talking to someone who thought that a girl went to college to meet a husband. I went to protest rallies because I liked the music. I bought a guitar because I thought it looked good on the bed! This life-style, this knowledge that you take for granted, was all a little out of left field for me.

ARTHUR

I can imagine.

MARION

No, I don't think you can. I met Collin in college, married him right after graduation and settled down for a nice quiet life of Kids and Careers. You think I had any idea about this? Talk about life's little surprises. You live with someone for sixteen years, you share your life, your bed, you have a child together, and then you wake up one day and he tells you that to him it's all been a lie. A lie. Try that on for size. Here you are the happiest couple you know, fulfilling your every life fantasy and he tells you he's living a lie.

ARTHUR

I'm sure he never said that.

MARION

Don't be so sure. There was a lot of new ground being broken back then and plenty of it was muddy.

ARTHUR

You know that he loved you.

MARION

What's that supposed to do, make things easier? It doesn't. I was brought up to believe, among other things, that if you had love that was enough. So what if I wasn't everything he wanted. Maybe he wasn't exactly everything I wanted either. So, you know what? You count your blessings and you settle.

ARTHUR

No one has to settle. Not him. Not you.

MARION

Of course not. You can say, "Up yours!" to everything and everyone who depends and needs you, and go off to make yourself happy.

ARTHUR

It's not that simple.

MARION

No. This is simpler. Death is simpler.
(*Yelling out*)
Happy now?

(THEY *stare at each other.* MARION *calms the rage and catches her breath.* ARTHUR *holds his emotions in check*)

ARTHUR
How about a nice hot cup of coffee? Tea with lemon?
Hot cocoa with a marshmallow floating in it?

MARION (*Laughs*)
I was wrong. You *are* a mother.

(ARTHUR *goes into the kitchen and starts preparing
things.* MARION *loafs by the doorway*)

MARION
I lied before. He *was* everything I ever wanted.

(ARTHUR *stops, looks at her, and then changes the
subject as* HE *goes on with his work*)

ARTHUR
When I came into the building and saw Jimmy in the
lobby I absolutely freaked for a second. It's amazing
how much they look alike. It was like seeing a little
miniature Collin standing there.

MARION
I know. He's like Collin's clone. There's nothing of me
in him.

ARTHUR
I always kinda hoped that when he grew up he'd take
after me. Not much chance, I guess.

MARION
Don't do anything fancy in there.

89

ARTHUR

Please. Anything we can consume is one less thing to pack.

MARION

So you've said.

ARTHUR

So *we've* said.

MARION

I want to keep seeing you and I want you to see Jim. You're still part of this family. No one's looking to cut you out.

ARTHUR

Ah, who'd want a kid to grow up looking like me anyway. I had enough trouble looking like this. Why pass on the misery?

MARION

You're adorable.

ARTHUR

Is that like saying I have a good personality?

MARION

I think you are one of the most naturally handsome men I know.

ARTHUR

Natural is right, and the bloom is fading.

MARION

All you need is a few good nights' sleep to kill those rings under your eyes.

ARTHUR

Forget the rings under my eyes,
          (*Grabbing his middle*)
. . . how about the rings around my moon?

MARION

I like you like this.

ARTHUR

From the time that Collin started using the wheelchair until he died, about six months, I lost twenty-three pounds. No gym, no diet. In the last seven weeks I've gained close to fifty.

MARION

You're exaggerating.

ARTHUR

I'd prove it on the bathroom scale, but I sold it in working order.

MARION

You'd never know.

ARTHUR

Marion, *you'd* never know, but ask my belt. Ask my pants. Ask my underwear. Even my stretch socks have stretch marks. I called the ambulance at five A.M., he was gone at nine and by nine-thirty, I was on a first-name basis with Sara Lee. I can quote the business hours of every ice-cream parlor, pizzeria and bakery on the island of Manhattan. I know the location of every twenty-four-hour grocery in the greater New York area, and I have memorized the phone numbers of every Mandarin, Szechuan and Hunan restaurant with free delivery.

MARION

At least you haven't wasted your time on useless hobbies.

ARTHUR

Are you kidding? I'm opening my own Overeater's Hotline. We'll have to start small, but expansion is guaranteed.

MARION

You're the best, you know that? If I couldn't be everything that Collin wanted then I'm grateful that he found someone like you.

ARTHUR
(*Turning on her without missing a beat*)
Keep your goddamned gratitude to yourself. I didn't go through any of this for you. So your thanks are out of line. And he didn't find "someone like" me. It was me.

MARION (*Frightened*)
I didn't mean . . .

ARTHUR
And I wish you'd remember one thing more: He died in my arms, not yours.

(MARION *is totally caught off guard.* SHE *stares disbelieving, openmouthed.* ARTHUR *walks past her as*

HE *leaves the kitchen with place mats.* HE *puts them on the coffee table. As* HE *arranges the papers and place mats* HE *speaks, never looking at her*)

ARTHUR

Look, I know you were trying to say something supportive. Don't waste your breath. There's nothing you can say that will make any of this easier for me. There's no way for you to help me get through this. And that's your fault. After three years you still have no idea or understanding of who I am. Or maybe you do know but refuse to accept it. I don't know and I don't care. But at least understand, from my point of view, who you are: You are my husband's *ex*-wife. If you like, the mother of *my* stepson. Don't flatter yourself into thinking you're any more than that. And whatever you are, you're certainly not my friend.

(HE *stops, looks up at her, then passes her again as* HE *goes back to the kitchen.*
MARION *is shaken, working hard to control herself.* SHE *moves toward the couch*)

MARION

Why don't we just sign these papers and I'll be out of your way.

ARTHUR

Shouldn't you say *I'll* be out of *your* way? After all, I'm not just signing papers, I'm signing away my home.

MARION
(*Resolved not to fight,* SHE *gets her purse*)

93

I'll leave the papers here. Please have them notarized
and returned to my lawyer.

ARTHUR

Don't forget my painting.

MARION (*Exploding*)

What do you want from me, Arthur?

ARTHUR (*Yelling back*)

I want you the hell out of my apartment! I want you
out of my life! And I want you to leave Collin alone!

MARION

The man's dead. I don't know how much more alone
I can leave him.

(ARTHUR *laughs at the irony, but behind the laughter
is something much more desperate*)

ARTHUR

Lots more, Marion. You've got to let him go.

MARION

For the life of me, I don't know what I did, or what
you think I did, for you to treat me like this. But you're
not going to get away with it. You will not take your
anger out on me. I will not stand here and be badgered
and insulted by you. I know you've been hurt and I
know you're hurting but you're not the only one who
lost someone here.

ARTHUR (*Topping her*)

Yes I am! You didn't just lose him. I did! You lost him

five years ago when he divorced you. This is not your
moment of grief and loss, it's mine!
(*Picking up the bundle of cards and throwing it toward
her*)
These condolences do not belong to you, they're mine.
(*Tossing her list back to her*)
His things are not yours to give away, they're mine!
This death does not belong to you, it's mine! Bought
and paid for outright. I suffered for it, I bled for it.
I was the one who cooked his meals. I was the one who
spoon-fed them. I pushed his wheelchair. I carried and
bathed him. I wiped his backside and changed his dia-
pers. I breathed life into and wrestled fear out of his
heart. I kept him alive for two years longer than any
doctor thought possible and when it was time I was the
one who prepared him for death.
I paid in full for my place in his life and I will *not* share
it with you. We are not the two widows of Collin Red-
ding. Your life was not here. Your husband didn't just
die. You've got a son and a life somewhere else. Your
husband's sitting, waiting for you at home, wondering,
as I am, what the hell you're doing here and why you
can't let go.

(MARION *leans back against the couch.* SHE*'s blown
away.* ARTHUR *stands staring at her*)

ARTHUR
(*Quietly*)
Let him go, Marion. He's mine. Dead or alive; mine.

(*The teakettle whistles.*
ARTHUR *leaves the room, goes to the kitchen and pours
the water as* MARION *pulls herself together.*

95

(ARTHUR *carries the loaded tray back into the living room and sets it down on the coffee table.* HE *sits and pours a cup*)

ARTHUR

One marshmallow or two?

(MARION *stares, unsure as to whether the attack is really over or not*)

ARTHUR
(*Placing them in her cup*)

Take three, they're small.

(MARION *smiles and takes the offered cup*)

ARTHUR
(*Campily*)

Now let me tell you how I *really* feel.

(MARION *jumps slightly, then* THEY *share a small laugh. Silence as* THEY *each gather themselves and sip their refreshments*)

MARION (*Calmly*)

Do you think that I sold the apartment just to throw you out?

ARTHUR

I don't care about the apartment . . .

MARION

. . . Because I really didn't. Believe me.

ARTHUR

I know.

MARION

I knew the expenses here were too much for you, and I knew you couldn't afford to buy out my half . . . I figured if we sold it, that you'd at least have a nice chunk of money to start over with.

ARTHUR

You could've given me a little more time.

MARION

Maybe. But I thought the sooner you were out of here, the sooner you could go on with your life.

ARTHUR

Or the sooner you could go on with yours.

MARION

Maybe.
                (Pause to gather her thoughts)
Anyway, I'm not going to tell you that I have no idea what you're talking about. I'd have to be worse than deaf and blind not to have seen the way you've been treated. Or mistreated. When I read Collin's obituary in the newspaper and saw my name and Jimmy's name and no mention of you . . .
                (Shakes her head, not knowing what to say)
You know that his secretary was the one who wrote that up and sent it in. Not me. But I should have done something about it and I didn't. I know.

ARTHUR

Wouldn't have made a difference. I wrote my own obituary for him and sent it to the smaller papers. They edited me out.

MARION

I'm sorry. I remember, at the funeral, I was surrounded by all of Collin's family and business associates while you were left with your friends. I knew it was wrong. I knew I should have said something but it felt good to have them around me and you looked like you were holding up . . . Wrong. But saying that it's all my fault for not letting go . . . ? There were other people involved.

ARTHUR

Who took their cue from you.

MARION

Arthur, you don't understand. Most people that we knew as a couple had no idea that Collin was Gay right up to his death. And even those that did know only found out when he got sick and the word leaked out that it was AIDS. I don't think I have to tell you how stupid and ill-informed most people are about homosexuality. And AIDS . . . ? The kinds of insane behavior that word inspires . . . ?

Those people at the funeral, how many times did they call to see how he was doing over these years? How many of them ever went to see him in the hospital? Did any of them even come here? So, why would you expect them to act any differently after his death?

So, maybe that helps to explain their behavior, but what about mine, right? Well, maybe there is no explanation. Only excuses. And excuse number one is that you're right, I have never really let go of him. And I am jealous of you. Hell, I was jealous of anyone that Collin ever talked to, let alone slept with . . . let alone loved.

The first year, after he moved out, we talked all the time about the different men he was seeing. And I always listened and advised. It was kind of fun. It kept us close. It kept me a part of his intimate life. And the bottom line was always that he wasn't happy with the men he was meeting. So, I was always allowed to hang on to the hope that one day he'd give it all up and come home. Then he got sick.

He called me, told me he was in the hospital and asked if I'd come see him. I ran. When I got to his door there was a sign, INSTRUCTIONS FOR VISITORS OF AN AIDS PATIENT. I nearly died.

ARTHUR

He hadn't told you?

MARION

No. And believe me, a sign is not the way to find these things out. I was so angry . . . And he was so sick . . . I was sure that he'd die right then. If not from the illness then from the hospital staff's neglect. No one wanted to go near him and I didn't bother fighting with them because I understood that they were scared. I was scared. That whole month in the hospital I didn't let Jimmy visit him once.

You learn.

Well, as you know, he didn't die. And he asked if he could come stay with me until he was well. And I said yes. Of course, yes. Now, here's something I never thought I'd ever admit to anyone: had he asked to stay with me for a few weeks I would have said no. But he asked to stay with me until he was well and knowing there was no cure I said yes. In my craziness I said yes because to me that meant forever. That he was coming back to me forever. Not that I wanted him to die, but I assumed from everything I'd read . . . And we'd be back together for whatever time he had left. Can you understand that?

(ARTHUR *nods*)

MARION
(*Gathers her thoughts again*)
Two weeks later he left. He moved in here. Into this apartment that we had bought as an investment. Never to live in. Certainly never to live apart in. Next thing I knew, the name Arthur starts appearing in every phone call, every dinner conversation.
"Did you see the doctor?"
"Yes. Arthur made sure I kept the appointment."
"Are you going to your folks for Thanksgiving?"
"No. Arthur and I are having some friends over."
I don't know which one of us was more of a coward, he for not telling or me for not asking about you. But eventually you became a given. Then, of course, we met and became what I had always thought of as friends.

(ARTHUR *winces in guilt*)

MARION
I don't care what you say, how could we not be friends with something so great in common: love for one of the most special human beings there ever was. And don't try and tell me there weren't times when you enjoyed my being around as an ally. I can think of a dozen

occasions when we ganged up on him, teasing him with
our intimate knowledge of his personal habits.

(ARTHUR *has to laugh*)

MARION

Blanket stealing? Snoring? Excess gas, no less?
(*Takes a moment to enjoy this truce*)
I don't think that my loving him threatened your re-
lationship. Maybe I'm not being truthful with myself.
But I don't. I never tried to step between you. Not that
I ever had the opportunity. Talk about being joined at
the hip! And that's not to say I wasn't jealous. I was.
Terribly. Hatefully. But always lovingly. I was happy
for Collin because there was no way to deny that he
was happy. With everything he was facing, he was happy.
Love did that. You did that.
He lit up with you. He came to life. I envied that and
all the time you spent together, but more, I watched
you care for him (sometimes *overcare* for him), and I
was in awe. I could never have done what you did. I
never would have survived. I really don't know how
you did.

ARTHUR

Who said I survived?

MARION

Don't tease. You did an absolutely incredible thing. It's
not as if you met him before he got sick. You entered
a relationship that you knew in all probability would
end this way and you never wavered.

ARTHUR

Of course I did. Don't have me sainted, Marion. But

sometimes you have no choice. Believe me, if I could've gotten away from him I would've. But I was a prisoner of love.

(HE *makes a campy gesture and pose*)

MARION

Stop.

ARTHUR

And there were lots of pluses. I got to quit a job I hated, stay home all day and watch game shows. I met a lot of doctors and learned a lot of big words.
    (ARTHUR *jumps up and goes to the pile of boxes where*
    HE *extracts one and brings it back to the couch*)
And then there was all the exciting traveling I got to do. This box has a souvenir from each one of our trips. Wanna see?

(MARION *nods.* HE *opens the box and pulls things out
one by one*)

ARTHUR (*Continued*)
(*Holding up an old bottle*)
This is from the house we rented in Reno when we went to clear out his lungs.
    (*Holding handmade potholders*)
This is from the hospital in Reno. Collin made them. They had a great arts and crafts program.
    (*Copper bracelets*)
These are from a faith healer in Philly. They don't do much for a fever, but they look great with a green sweater.
    (*Glass ashtrays*)

These are from our first visit to the clinic in France.
Such lovely people.

>*(A Bible)*

This is from our second visit to the clinic in France.

>*(A bead necklace)*

A Voodoo doctor in New Orleans. Next time we'll have
to get there earlier in the year. I think he sold all the
pretty ones at Mardi Gras.

>*(A tiny piñata)*

Then there was Mexico. Black market drugs and empty
wallets.

>*(Now pulling things out at random)*

L.A., San Francisco, Houston, Boston . . . We traveled
everywhere they offered hope for sale and came home
with souvenirs.

>*(ARTHUR quietly pulls a few more things out and then
begins to put them all back into the box slowly. Softly
as HE works:)*

Marion, I would have done anything, traveled anywhere
to avoid . . . or delay . . . Not just because I loved him
so desperately, but when you've lived the way we did
for three years . . . the battle becomes your life.

>*(HE looks at her and then away)*

His last few hours were beyond any scenario I had imag-
ined. He hadn't walked in nearly six months. He was
totally incontinent. If he spoke two words in a week I
was thankful. Days went by without his eyes ever fo-
cusing on me. He just stared out at I don't know what.
Not the meals as I fed him. Not the TV I played con-
stantly for company. Just out. Or maybe in.
It was the middle of the night when I heard his breathing
become labored. His lungs were filling with fluid again.
I knew the sound. I'd heard it a hundred times before.
So, I called the ambulance and got him to the hospital.

They hooked him up to the machines, the oxygen, shot him with morphine and told me that they would do what they could to keep him alive.

But, Marion, it wasn't the machines that kept him breathing. He did it himself. It was that incredible will and strength inside him. Whether it came from his love of life or fear of death, who knows. But he'd been counted out a hundred times and a hundred times he fought his way back.

I got a magazine to read him, pulled a chair up to the side of his bed and holding his hand, I wondered whether I should call Helen to let the cleaning lady in or if he'd fall asleep and I could sneak home for an hour. I looked up from the page and he was looking at me. Really looking right into my eyes. I patted his cheek and said, "Don't worry, honey, you're going to be fine."

But there was something else in his eyes. He wasn't satisfied with that. And I don't know why, I have no idea where it came from, I just heard the words coming out of my mouth, "Collin, do you want to die?"

His eyes filled and closed, he nodded his head.

I can't tell you what I was thinking, I'm not sure I was. I slipped off my shoes, lifted his blanket and climbed into bed next to him. I helped him to put his arms around me, and mine around him, and whispered as gently as I could into his ear, "It's alright to let go now. It's time to go on." And he did.

Marion, you've got your life and his son. All I have is an intangible place in a man's history. Leave me that. Respect that.

MARION

I understand.

(ARTHUR *suddenly comes to life, running to get the shopping bag that* HE'*d left at the front door*)

ARTHUR

Jeez! With all the screamin' and sad storytelling I forget something.
(HE *extracts a bouquet of flowers from the bag*)
I brung you flowers and everything.

MARION

You brought *me* flowers?

ARTHUR

Well, I knew you'd never think to bring me flowers and I felt that on an occasion such as this somebody oughta get flowers from somebody.

MARION

You know, Arthur, you're really making me feel like a worthless piece of garbage.

ARTHUR

So what else is new?
(HE *presents the flowers*)
Just promise me one thing: Don't press one in a book. Just stick them in a vase and when they fade just toss them out. No more memorabilia.

MARION

Arthur, I want to do something for you and I don't know what. Tell me what you want.

ARTHUR

I want little things. Not much. I want to be remembered. If you get a Christmas card from Collin's mother, make sure she sent me one too. If his friends call to see how you are, ask if they've called me. Have me to dinner so I can see Jimmy. Let me take him out now and then. Invite me to his wedding.

(THEY BOTH *laugh*)

MARION
You've got it.

ARTHUR (*Clearing the table*)
Let me get all this cold cocoa out of the way. We still have the deed to do.

MARION (*Checking her watch*)
And I've got to get Jimmy home in time for practice.

ARTHUR
Band practice?

MARION
Baseball.
(*Picking her list off the floor*)
About this list, you do what you want.

ARTHUR
Believe me, I will. But I promise to consider your suggestions. Just don't rush me. I'm not ready to give it all away.
(ARTHUR *is off to the kitchen with his tray and the phone rings.* HE *answers it in the kitchen*)
Hello? . . . Just a minute.
(*Calling out*)
It's your eager Little Leaguer.

(MARION *picks up the living room extension and AR-THUR hangs his up*)

MARION (*Into phone*)
Hello, honey. . . . I'll be down in five minutes. No.
You know what? You come up here and get me. . . . No,
I said you should come up here. . . . I said I want to
come up here. . . . Because I said so. . . . Thank you.

(SHE *hangs the receiver*)

ARTHUR (*Rushing to the papers*)
Alright, where do we start on these?

MARION (*Getting out her seal*)
I guess you should just start signing everything and I'll
stamp along with you. Keep one of everything on the
side for yourself.

ARTHUR
Now I feel so rushed. What am I signing?

MARION
You want to do this another time?

ARTHUR
No. Let's get it over with. I wouldn't survive another
session like this.

(HE *starts to sign and* SHE *starts her job*)

MARION
I keep meaning to ask you; how are you?

ARTHUR
(*At first puzzled and then:*)
Oh, you mean my health? Fine: No, I'm fine. I've been
tested, and nothing. We were very careful. We took
many precautions. Collin used to make jokes about how
we should invest in rubber futures.

MARION
I'll bet.

ARTHUR (*Stops what* HE's *doing*)
It never occurred to me until now. How about you?

MARION (*Not stopping*)
Well, we never had sex after he got sick.

ARTHUR
But before?

MARION
(*Stopping but not looking up*)
I have the antibodies in my blood. No signs that it will
ever develop into anything else. And it's been five years
so my chances are pretty good that I'm just a carrier.

ARTHUR
I'm so sorry. Collin never told me.

MARION
He didn't know. In fact, other than my husband and
the doctors, you're the only one I've told.

ARTHUR
You and your husband . . . ?

MARION

Have invested in rubber futures. There'd only be a problem if we wanted to have a child. Which we do. But we'll wait. Miracles happen every day.

ARTHUR

I don't know what to say.

MARION

Tell me you'll be there if I ever need you.

(ARTHUR *gets up, goes to her and puts his arms around her.* THEY *hold each other.* HE *gently pushes her away to make a joke*)

ARTHUR

Sure! Take something else that should have been mine.

MARION

Don't even joke about things like that.

(*The doorbell rings.* THEY *pull themselves together*)

ARTHUR

You know we'll never get these done today.

MARION

So, tomorrow.

(ARTHUR *goes to open the door as* MARION *gathers her things.* HE *opens the door and* JIMMY *is standing in the hall*)

JIM

C'mon, Ma. I'm gonna be late.

ARTHUR

Would you like to come inside?

JIM

We've gotta go.

MARION

Jimmy, come on.

JIM

Ma!

(SHE *glares.* HE *comes in.* ARTHUR *closes the door*)

MARION (*Holding out the flowers*)

Take these for Mommy.

JIM (*Taking them*)

Can we go?

MARION (*Picking up the painting*)

Say good-bye to your Uncle Arthur.

JIM

'Bye, Arthur. Come on.

MARION

Give him a kiss.

ARTHUR

Marion, don't.

MARION

Give your uncle a kiss good-bye.

JIM

He's not my uncle.

MARION

No. He's a hell of a lot more than your uncle.

ARTHUR (*Offering his hand*)

A handshake will do.

MARION

Tell Uncle Arthur what your daddy told you.

JIM

About what?

MARION

Stop playing dumb. You know.

ARTHUR

Don't embarrass him.

MARION

Jimmy, please.

JIM

(HE *regards his* MOTHER's *softer tone and then speaks*)

He said that after me and Mommy he loved you the
most.

111

MARION (*Standing behind him*)
Go on.

JIM
And that I should love you too. And make sure that you're not lonely or very sad.

ARTHUR
Thank you.

(ARTHUR *reaches down to the* BOY *and* THEY *hug.* JIM *gives him a little peck on the cheek and then breaks away*)

MARION (*Going to open the door*)
Alright, kid, you done good. Now let's blow this joint before you muck it up.

(JIM *rushes out the door.* MARION *turns to* ARTHUR)

MARION
A child's kiss is magic. Why else would they be so stingy with them. I'll call you.

(ARTHUR *nods understanding.* MARION *pulls the door closed behind her.*
ARTHUR *stands quietly as the lights fade to black*)

THE END

NOTE: *If being performed on film, the final image should be of* ARTHUR *leaning his back against the closed door on the inside of the apartment and* MARION *leaning on the outside of the door. A moment of thought and then* THEY BOTH *move on.*

Harvey Fierstein made his playwriting debut in 1973 with *In Search of the Cobra Jewels,* followed by *Freaky Pussy* and *Flatbush Tosca.* During the 1978 and 1979 seasons La Mama E.T.C. presented *International Stud, Fugue in a Nursery* and *Widows and Children First!,* the plays which make up *Torch Song Trilogy.* The Glines Inc. presented *Torch Song* in 1981, transferring the production to Broadway in 1982, earning Fierstein the Theatre World Award, the Best Actor Tony Award and the Best Actor Drama Desk Award. *Torch Song Trilogy* was also named Best Play in 1983 by the Tony and Drama Desk Awards. Recipient, as well, of the Hull Warriner Award from the Dramatists Guild, the Oppenheimer/Newsday Award, the Obie/Village Voice Award and the Fund for Human Dignity Award, in addition to grants from the Rockefeller Foundation, The Ford Foundation and CAPS, Fierstein received his third Tony Award for the book for the stage musical *La Cage aux Folles.* His other plays include *Forget Him* and *Spookhouse.*